101 AMAZING FACTS ABOUT

Dogs

LEARN MORE ABOUT MAN'S BEST FRIEND

Jenny Kellett

BELLANOVA

MELBOURNE · SOFIA · BERLIN

101 Amazing Facts About Dogs
www.bellanovabooks.com

Paperback
ISBN: 978-619-7695-95-3
Imprint: Bellanova Books

Contents

INTRODUCTION

It's hard not to love dogs, in fact 1 in 3 American families have at least one pooch! But how much do you know about your puppy or dog?

In this book you will learn over 100 amazing new things about your best friend. From the huge Great Dane to the tiny Chihuahua, you'll be a cynologist (a dog expert) in no time!

Are you ready? *Let's go!*

King Charles spaniel.

Dogs:
THE FACTS

Dogs are mentioned 14 times in the Bible.

• • •

City dogs live three years longer than a country dog, on average.

• • •

In 1957, a dog named Laika was launched into space on the Russian spacecraft Sputnik 2.

Australian kelpie

The Australian kelpie is an intelligent and friendly breed, which is used to muster livestock such as sheep.

Old English sheepdog

The Old English sheepdog is a very friendly, but incredibly furry dog. Their coats need regular brushing as they can't shed their fur on their own.

Dalmatians are born completely white.

. . .

Dogs don't like the rain because the sound is too
loud for their ears.

. . .

Border collies and poodles are considered to
be the smartest dog breeds, whereas Afghan
hounds and the basenji are the least intelligent.

. . .

The *Taco Bell* Chihuahua is a rescued dog
named Gidget.

Golden retriever

Golden retrievers are famous for their affectionate nature and are one of the world's most popular dog breeds.

The oldest dog on record was an Australian cattle dog called Bluey who lived until he was 29 years old.

• • •

In seven years, one female dog and her female offspring could produce 4,372 puppies!

• • •

Dogs only have sweat glands in between their paw pads - nowhere else.

• • •

Some studies have shown that dogs can detect cancer by smelling a person's breath.

Greyhounds can run up to 45 miles an hour (72 km/h)!

• • •

The real name of Toto the dog in the movie *Wizard of Oz* was Terry.

• • •

The smallest dog on record was a Yorkshire terrier from Great Britain who, at the age of two, weighed just four ounces (113 g).

• • •

If you spay/neuter your dog before it turns six months old, you can lower its risk of getting cancer.

Spanish galgo

The galgo is very closely related to the greyhound and they are often cross-bred.

Afghan hound

The Afghan hound comes from the cold mountain regions of Afghanistan, where it relies on its long, warm coat.

Female dogs carry their puppies for about 60 days before they are born.

• • •

Davy Crockett had a dog named *Sport*.

• • •

A dog's level of intelligence is equivalent to that of a human two year old.

• • •

A dog's heart beat is between 70 and 120 pulses a minute. A human's heart beats between 70 and 80 times a minute.

The most popular names for a male dog are Max and Jake. The most popular female names are Maggie and Molly.

• • •

The highest dog population in the world is in the USA. France comes second.

• • •

A dog's sense of smell is 100,000 times stronger than that of humans.

• • •

A dog's ear has over 18 muscles in it.

French bulldog

The French bulldog
is a cross between
a bulldog and
a terrier. It
originated in
England and is
one of a few
dog breeds that
can't swim.

Rottweiler

Rottweilers originated in Germany and are commonly used as guard dogs. They are named after the town of Rottweil in Germany.

Dogs were the first animals domesticated by humans.

•••

The shape of a dog's face can help predict how long it will live.

•••

A dog's nose has over 200 scent-receiving cells.

•••

George Washington had 36 dogs — all foxhounds.

Every year, 15 people in the USA die from dog bites.

• • •

There are different smells in a dog's urine, which tells other dogs whether that dog is male or female, old or young, and sick or healthy.

• • •

Just like human babies, Chihuahua puppies are born with a soft spot in their skull which closes up with age.

Labradoodle

The labradoodle is a cross between a labrador and a poodle.

Dalmatian

No two dalmatians have the same pattern.

Even just small quantities of grapes, raisins and
chocolates can cause serious illness for your
dog.

• • •

People who own pets are said to live longer,
have less stress and have fewer heart attacks.

• • •

Dog nose prints are as unique as human
fingerprints and can be used to identify them.

• • •

Studies show that petting a dog can lower your
blood pressure.

Apple and pear seeds contain a chemical called arsenic, which can be deadly to dogs.

• • •

More than 1 in 3 American families own a dog.

• • •

Greyhounds have the best eyesight of any breed of dog.

• • •

Adult dogs have 42 teeth.

Maltipoo

They are a
cross between
the Maltese and
the poodle.

Siberian husky puppy

Siberian huskies can be difficult to keep as pets, as they are famous for their Houdini-like escape skills.

Around 80% of dog owners give their dogs gifts on holidays such as Christmas and birthdays.

. . .

Dogs' shoulder blades are not attached to their skeletons, allowing them to run quickly.

. . .

The first sense puppies develop is touch.

. . .

Dogs have twice as many muscles in their ears than humans.

Lundehund dogs have six toes on each foot!

• • •

Despite what many people think, dogs are not colorblind. However, they don't see colors as vividly as humans.

• • •

Prairie dogs actually belong to the squirrel family.

• • •

Just as humans can save lives by donating blood, dogs can do the same! If they share the same blood type, a dogs blood can be used to save another one.

Pomsky

The pomsky is a cross between a Pomeranian and a Siberian husky.

Dogs can understand up to 250 words and gestures and can do basic mathematical calculations.

• • •

Some stray dogs in Russia have worked out how to use the subway system to help them get around and find food.

• • •

The Beatles song *'A day in the life'* was recorded with a high-pitched whistle playing in the background that only dogs can hear!

Yorkshire terrier

The Yorkshire terrier's fur has a similar texture to human hair.

Pug

Pugs are one of the world's oldest dog breeds and have long been connected to royalty.

Seeing Eye dogs wee and poo on demand, so
that their owners know when to clean up after
them.

•••

Hyenas are more closely related to cats than
dogs.

•••

Spiked dog collars were invented in
Ancient Greece to protect dogs from
wolf attacks.

•••

Dogs drink water by forming the
back of their tongues into a mini cup.

In the USA, over 1 million dog owners have put their dog as the main beneficiary of their will!

• • •

Dogs have three eyelids.

• • •

The basenji is the world's only dog that doesn't bark.

• • •

There are an estimated 400 million dogs in the world.

Basenji

The basenji is an ancient breed native to central Africa. It has a lightly wrinkled head and pointy ears.

Border collie

Border collies are incredibly smart—in fact, they are believed to be the smartest dog breed in existence, and can learn a huge number of words and commands.

Around 33% of dog owners have admitted to talking to their dogs on the phone, some even leave them voice mails!

• • •

There are hundreds of different breeds of dog, which are divided into eight different classes: sporting, hound, terrier, working, herding, non-sporting and miscellaneous.

• • •

All dogs are descendants of wolves.

• • •

Two dogs survived the sinking of the Titanic — a Pomeranian and a Pekingese.

West Highland terrier

Also known as the "Westie", the West Highland terrier originated in the rocky regions of Scotland after which they are named. They make great pets as they are very loyal.

Approximately 45% of dogs sleep in their owners bed!

. . .

Dogs curl up in a ball when they sleep to keep themselves warm and protect themselves from predators.

. . .

While chow chow dogs are famous for their blue-black tongues, they are actually born with pink tongues. Their tongues change color when they are around 8-10 weeks old.

. . .

Puppies get their full set of permanent teeth between four and six months old.

Dogs don't have an appendix.

• • •

Despite what many people think, the Canary Islands (a group of islands off the east coast of Africa) weren't named after birds, they were named after the large dogs that lived on the islands.

• • •

Domestic dogs are omnivores. This means they eat meat, grains and vegetables.

Chocolate labrador

Around 23.8% of labradors born are chocolate; 44.6% are black and 27.8% are yellow.

Weimaraner

The Weimarener was originally bred as a hunting dog in the early 19th century.

Dogs bark for a large number of reasons, but often do so to get attention from other people or other dogs. Some other reasons that dogs bark include: to protect their territory, express a need or to initiate play.

• • •

Dogs ears move independently of one another.

• • •

In their first few weeks of life, puppies spend 90% of each day sleeping.

• • •

Chihuahuas were named after the state in Mexico where they were discovered.

The Irish wolfhound is the world's tallest breed of dog.

• • •

Four out of five dogs over the age of three have gum disease.

• • •

Dogs can smell when you are sick.

• • •

When you smile at your dog with your teeth showing, they don't see it as a smile - they see it as a sign of aggression.

Great Dane

Along with its relative, the Irish wolfhound, the Great Dane is one of the largest dog breeds in the world.

Pomeranian

Pomeranians may look small, but they weren't always that way. They actually descended from large sled dogs.

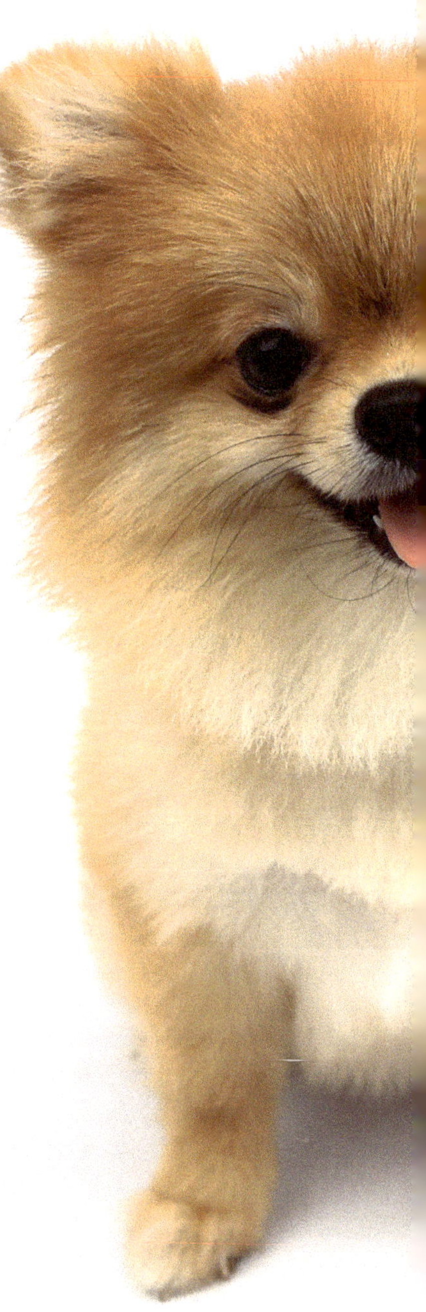

President Lyndon Johnson had two dogs named 'Him' and 'Her'.

...

Basset hounds cannot swim.

...

The Saint Bernard is, on average, the heaviest dog breed.

...

There are 6.2 million puppies born each year in the USA. In comparison, only 4 million human babies are born each year.

When a puppy turns one year old it is an adult. In human years, this is around 15 years old.

• • •

Puppies start off with 28 teeth before they get their full adult set of 42.

• • •

Dogs have a special membrane in their eyes that allows them to see in the dark.

• • •

Dogs pant to cool themselves off.

Dobermann

The Dobermann, known as the Doberman-Pinscher in the US and Canada, is a highly intelligent German dog breed. They are often used as security and police dogs as they can become aggressive. If they are kept as pets they need to be very well trained.

Boxer

Boxers are very loving dogs and are popular with families. They were first introduced into the United States after World War I, but didn't become popular until the late 1930s.

When dogs kick after going to the toilet, they do it to spread their scent as far as possible.

• • •

Based on the average life span of 11 years, the cost of owning a dog is around $13,500.

• • •

A dog's whiskers are touch-sensitive hairs called *vibrissae*. They are found on the muzzle, above the eyes and below the jaws, and can sense tiny changes in airflow.

• • •

Smaller breeds of dog mature faster than larger breeds.

Dogs with deep wrinkles need to be washed daily. Dirt can build up leading to odor or infection.

• • •

Dogs often react differently to human males and females.

• • •

Some dogs lick their paws and then rub their paws on their head to clean themselves, much like a cat!

• • •

Dogs can get jealous. They may try and interrupt a hugging couple or bark for attention when you are on the telephone!

Maltese

The Maltese dog is one of the
oldest breeds in the world.
Aristotle described
the Maltese as
"perfectly
proportioned".

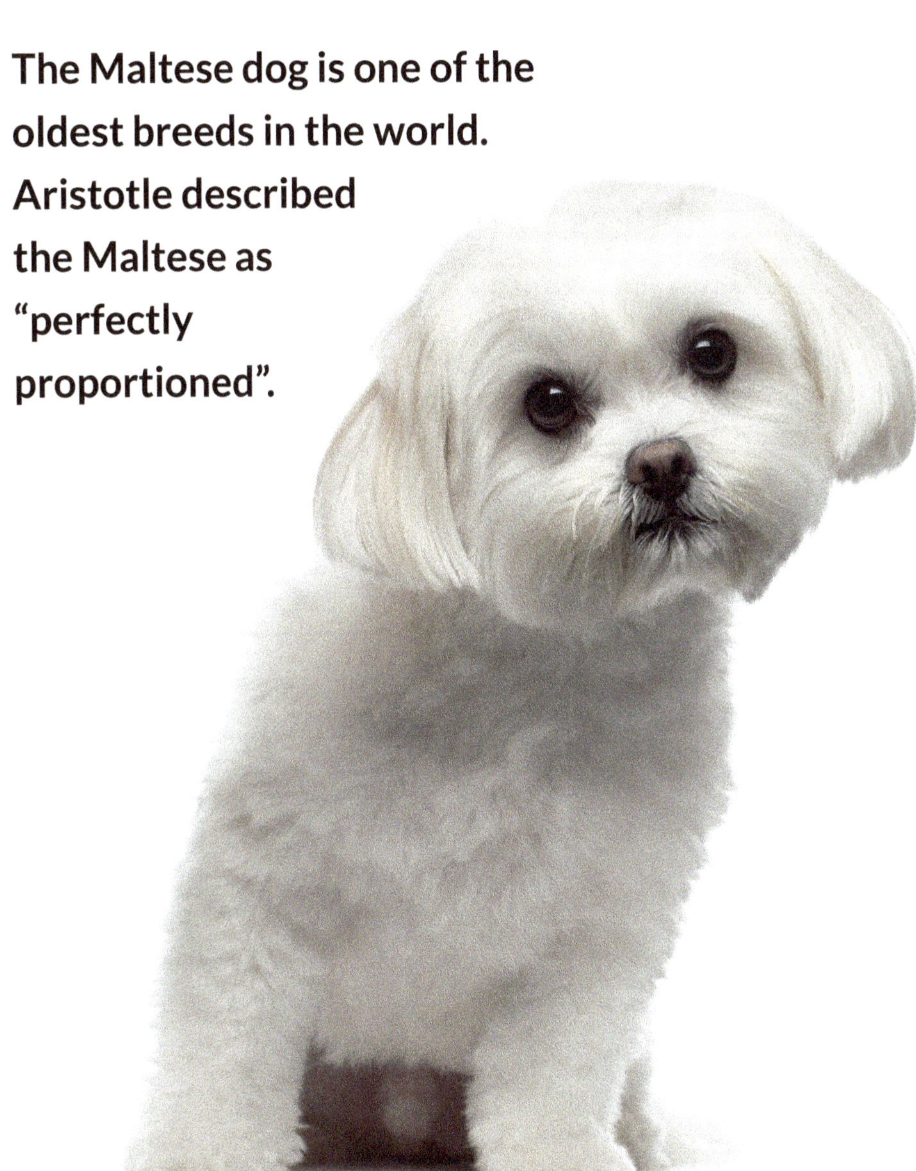

Corgi

The word 'corgi' comes from the Welsh words 'cor', meaning dwarf, and 'gi', meaning dog.

Teddy Roosevelt's dog, Pete, ripped a French ambassador's pants off at the White House!

• • •

Obesity is the number one health problem among dogs.

• • •

Dogs have no sense of "time".

• • •

Cynophobia is the fear of dogs.

• • •

A person who loves dogs is called a canophilist!

Only dogs and humans have prostates.

• • •

Dachshunds were originally bred for fighting badgers.

• • •

Dogs judge objects first by their movement, then by their brightness, and lastly by their shape.

• • •

All dogs are identical in anatomy - they all have 321 bones.

Dachshund

Also known as a "sausage dog", the breed came before the hot dog was invented. In fact, the hot dog was originally called a "Dachshund sausage".

DOGS
WORD SEARCH

C	H	I	H	U	A	H	U	A	A	P	D
D	Y	E	S	F	H	K	Q	W	S	O	Y
M	A	L	T	E	S	E	Z	W	D	M	T
N	R	C	A	N	I	N	E	P	O	E	R
B	T	S	H	B	N	H	G	L	G	R	H
D	K	Q	W	S	Z	X	F	A	R	A	G
P	J	E	U	Y	H	B	V	B	D	N	S
U	B	G	L	S	D	U	E	R	K	I	F
P	B	T	Z	P	W	E	N	A	R	A	B
P	J	H	G	D	I	V	C	D	D	N	V
Y	T	E	R	R	I	E	R	O	S	A	C
B	H	G	F	X	S	Z	N	R	N	H	Z

Can you find all the words below in the wordsearch puzzle on the left?

MALTESE	POMERANIAN	CANINE
DACHSHUND	LABRADOR	KELPIE
TERRIER	CHIHUAHUA	PUPPY

SOLUTION

C	H	I	H	U	A	H	U	A		P	
D										O	
M	A	L	T	E	S	E				M	
		C	A	N	I	N	E			E	
		H						L		R	
	K		S					A		A	
P		E		H				B		N	
U		L		U				R		I	
P			P			N		A		A	
P				I				D		N	
Y	T	E	R	R	I	E	R	O			
								R			

SOURCES

"Dog Facts". 2022. American Kennel Club. https://www.akc.org/expert-advice/lifestyle/dog-facts/.

"42 Amazing Facts About Dogs". 2019. Mental Floss. https://www.mentalfloss.com/article/564264/dogs-puppies-facts.

"52 Fun Facts About Dogs". 2022. Reader's Digest. https://www.rd.com/list/dog-facts-you-didnt-know/.

"Dog Facts". 2022. Natgeo Kids. https://www.natgeokids.com/uk/discover/animals/general-animals/dog-facts/.

"Amazing facts about dogs". 2021. The Wildest. https://www.thewildest.com/dog-behavior/amazing-facts-about-dogs.

"Dog | History, Domestication, Physical Traits, Breeds, & Facts". 2022. Encyclopedia Britannica. https://www.britannica.com/animal/dog.

"Dog - Wikipedia". 2022. En.Wikipedia.Org. https://en.wikipedia.org/wiki/Dog.

"Great Dane - Wikipedia". 2015. En.Wikipedia.Org. https://en.wikipedia.org/wiki/Great_Dane.

"Saint Bernard - Wikipedia". 2022. En.Wikipedia. Org. https://en.wikipedia.org/wiki/Saint_Bernard.

"30 Unique Dog Breeds You've Never Heard Of— Until Now". 2022. Reader's Digest Canada. https://www.readersdigest.ca/home-garden/pets/10-unique-dog-breeds/.

"Things you didn't know about the dachshund". 2022. American Kennel Club. https://www.akc.org/expert-advice/lifestyle/things-you-didnt-know-about-the-dachshund/.

"Boxer facts you might not know". 2022. American Kennel Club. https://www.akc.org/expert-advice/lifestyle/boxer-facts-you-might-not-know/.

AND THAT'S ALL, FOLKS!

We'd love it if you left us a **review**—they always make us smile, but more importantly they help other readers make better buying decisions.

Visit us at:

www.bellanovabooks.com

**for more fun fact books
and regular giveaways!**

ALSO BY JENNY KELLETT

... and more!

Available at

www.bellanovabooks.com

and all major online
bookstores.